Silly Shakespeare for Students

I0517932

OTHELLO

PAUL LEONARD MURRAY

with help from

WILLIAM SHAKESPEARE

Alphabet PUBLISHING

ISBN: 978-1-956159-51-6 (paperback)
ISBN: 978-1-956159-52-3 (ebook)

For permission requests or discounts on class sets and bulk orders contact us at:

Alphabet Publishing
29 Milo Drive
Branford, CT 06405 USA

info@alphabetpublishingbooks.com
www.alphabetpublishingbooks.com

For performance rights, please contact Paul Murray at paulplaying@gmail.com

Interior Formatting and Cover Design by Melissa Williams Design

For Anja and Izabela

The Story Behind Shakespeare's Othello

Imagine a world where power, honour, and social status are everything. That's the world of *Othello*, set in the 16th century. The play starts in Venice, a bustling city known for its political power and rich history. However, most of the action actually takes place on the island of Cyprus, which is just as intriguing and full of drama.

Origins of the Play

Believed to have been written in 1603, *Othello* is said to be inspired by a short story titled "Un Capitano Moro" (A Moorish Captain) by the Italian writer Giovanni Battista Giraldi, published in 1565. Shakespeare likely encountered this tale in one of the many collections of stories available at the time. The play reflects the cultural tensions of the Elizabethan era, particularly regarding race and identity, as Othello is a Black man navigating a predominantly white Venetian society. Shakespeare's adaptation deepens the themes of jealousy, manipulation, and the complexities of love, elevating the narrative beyond its origins to create a profound tragedy that resonates with audiences across generations.

The Plot

The story begins in Venice, where Iago is bitter because Othello has promoted Cassio over him. Iago feels slighted and harbours a deep grudge against Othello, believing he's been wronged in favour of Cassio. To make matters worse, Iago suspects that Othello might be having an affair with his wife, Emilia. Fueled by these feelings, Iago concocts a plan to ruin Othello's life.

Iago's plan kicks off with him convincing Roderigo, who is desperately in love with Othello's wife, Desdemona, to help him take revenge on Othello. Iago tells Roderigo that Desdemona will soon tire of Othello and return to him, so Roderigo agrees to help Iago in his schemes.

The play moves to Cyprus, where Othello and his entourage are sent to defend the island from a Turkish invasion. While they are there, Iago begins his psychological warfare against Othello. He manipulates events to make it appear as if Desdemona is being unfaithful to Othello with Cassio.

Iago's plan involves planting seeds of doubt in Othello's mind. He uses Desdemona's handkerchief, a special gift from Othello, to create false evidence of her infidelity. Iago tells Othello that he saw Cassio with the handkerchief, further convincing Othello of Desdemona's betrayal.

Othello, overwhelmed by jealousy and anger, becomes increasingly erratic and suspicious. His love for Desdemona turns to bitter resentment as he believes she has been unfaithful. Iago's manipulations are so effective that Othello loses trust in those around him, including his beloved wife.

Desdemona, unaware of the storm brewing, remains loyal and loving, trying to understand why Othello is so distant and hostile. Emilia, who is trying to help Desdemona, is also unwittingly drawn into Iago's deceptions.

As Othello's jealousy consumes him, he decides that the only way to resolve his anguish is to kill Desdemona. Iago continues to fuel Othello's rage, making the plan seem like the only solution to the perceived betrayal. Despite Desdemona's pleas and innocence, Othello strangles her in their bed.

The truth begins to unravel when Emilia discovers the tragic murder and reveals Iago's manipulations. Othello realizes too late that he has been deceived and that

Desdemona was faithful all along. Overcome with guilt and grief, Othello takes his own life.

Themes and Characters

1. **Othello**: The protagonist and a highly respected military leader. He's a Moor, meaning he's of North African descent, which makes him stand out in Venetian society.

2. **Desdemona**: Othello's loving and loyal wife. She's the daughter of a Venetian nobleman, Brabantio.

3. **Iago**: Othello's ensign (a lower-ranking officer), and the main antagonist of the play. Iago is cunning and manipulative, driven by jealousy and a desire for revenge.

4. **Cassio**: Othello's loyal lieutenant, who is well-liked but becomes a target of Iago's schemes.

5. **Emilia**: Iago's wife and Desdemona's maid. She is more important than she first appears, especially in relation to Iago's plans.

6. **Brabantio**: Desdemona's father, who is initially enraged by her secret marriage to Othello.

7. **Roderigo**: A wealthy Venetian who is in love with Desdemona and is manipulated by Iago.

Othello is a story about the destructive power of jealousy and the devastating effects of deceit. Iago's manipulation and Othello's unchecked jealousy lead to tragic consequences, underscoring the importance of trust and communication in relationships. The play highlights how easily trust can be shattered by lies and how destructive unchecked emotions can be.

The Play's Impact and Legacy

Othello has had a profound impact on literature and theatre since its creation, influencing countless adaptations across various media, including film, opera, and modern novels. The play's exploration of themes such as jealousy, race, and manipulation resonate with contemporary audiences, prompting discussions about identity and societal prejudices. Characters like Othello and Iago have become archetypes in literature, representing the complexities of human nature and the darker sides of ambition and deceit. The play also raises critical questions about trust and betrayal, making it relevant in today's context of personal and societal relationships. Academic discussions around *Othello* continue to examine issues of race and gender, enhancing its legacy as a work that challenges audiences to reflect on moral and ethical dilemmas. Overall, Shakespeare's *Othello* remains a vital part of the canon, celebrated for its emotional depth and intricate characterizations.

Playing Style

This version of *Othello*, although reduced to around a one-hour and fifteen minutes playing time, remains true to the original's plot, characters (with some small exceptions), and structure. When performed, this production should maintain a lively pace and exaggerated style.

Technically, the production, as with the original, has a very low level of technical requirements. The sets can be very minimal and the costumes simple. A musical score may be used between scenes to cover changes where necessary.

Of course, one of the major differences between this version and the original is the simplification of the text. On some occasions, in performance, you will find the rhyming scheme helpful to the playing, in which case the actors should just 'stand back', enjoy the words and help the audience do the same. On other occasions, the rhyming scheme will seem stifling and restrictive, in which case do not be afraid to improvise a little, add your own occasional lines or do not emphasise the rhymes so much.

Overall, this version while maintaining the tragedy and pathos of the original should also be fun to play and watch. It can be produced with a small budget and should be done 'over the top' which can give you a chance to play with your own ideas of theatricality.

Cast of Characters

OTHELLO
BRABANTIO
MONTANO
LODOVICO
CASSIO
IAGO
RODERIGO
DUKE of Venice
BIANCA
GRATIANO
DESDEMONA
EMILIA
Herald
Messengers
Senators
Gentlemen

Prologue

[Each character is posed on the stage. They come to life when they speak, except for IAGO, who is our narrator.]

IAGO

Welcome to Venice, a watery place,

Where starts the tale of my disgrace.

Iago's my name, but this play's called Othello,

[Points to OTHELLO] Named after this man, an insecure
fellow.

OTHELLO

But a very good general . . .

IAGO

    and stood next to him

[Points to CASSIO] is Cassio, his Lieutenant.

CASSIO

    I'm handsome . . .

IAGO

    but dim.

And Othello's girl here! *[Points to DESDEMONA]* Well, he
   doesn't yet 'own' her!

DESDEMONA
I'm honest, I'm pure, and my name's Desdemona.

IAGO
[Points to EMILIA] This is Emilia, her bestie for life,

EMILIA
Who also happens to be Iago's wife!

IAGO
[Points to BIANCA] Bianca is 'a girl of the night',
Who loves young Cassio,

BIANCA
   which won't help his plight!

IAGO
[Points to BRABANTIO] And Dessie's dad, Brabantio,

BRABANTIO
Who tries, but fails, to run the show.

IAGO
[Points to RODERIGO] And Roderigo, a Lord

RODERIGO
   who fancies his *[points at BRABANTIO]* daughter,

IAGO
And who I lead around like a lamb to the slaughter.
[Points to MONTANO] Montano of Cyprus . . .

MONTANO
> Who's the gov. of the isle

IAGO
[Points to the DUKE] And a Venetian Duke . . .

DUKE
> You will meet in a while.

IAGO
Brabantio's brothers are the last in the herd.

> *[Points to GRATIANO and LODOVICO]*

Gratiano and Lodovico, who will get the last word.

IAGO
This is the cast and you'll witness their deeds.
You'll see a few others, but these are leads.
Our story begins with me in hot water
As Rod's heard some news about Brabantio's daughter.

> *[All exeunt but RODERIGO AND IAGO]*

Act I

Scene I.

Night. In the street where Desdemona lives with her father, Brabantio.

[RODERIGO and IAGO are walking up the street.]

RODERIGO
You double-crossing little cur!
You said you'd set me up with her.
I gave you some cash like a good, trusting fellow.
Now I hear she's gone and hooked up with Othello!

IAGO
It didn't quite all go to plan.
Othello's my boss! But I too hate the man.
He overlooked me for promotion!

RODERIGO
A hasty and an unwise notion.

IAGO
He charmed poor Desdemona well,
But Othello's life we'll now make hell.

RODERIGO
He's very strong. Is it wise to attack?

IAGO
We'll do it all behind his back.
Just stick with me; do what I say.
My sneakiness will win the day!

[They stop walking and look at Brabantio's house.]

RODERIGO
Isn't this Brabantio's place?

IAGO
Indeed it is. Now open your face!

*[They start shouting, telling Brabantio to wake up because
he has been robbed.]*

IAGO AND RODERIGO
Robbery, thievery, your house is undone!

[Enter BRABANTIO]

BRABANTIO
What's all this noise? It's twenty past one!

IAGO
I know it's late but the news is bad.

RODERIGO

Your daughter's escaped and married a cad.

BRABANTIO

[Rubbing his tired eyes] Roderigo, is that you? Are you on your own?

I told you to leave Desdemona alone!

IAGO

[Whispering to RODERIGO] I'll leave it to you to explain what's amiss.

I can't be seen plotting against Othello like this.

[Exit IAGO]

RODERIGO

Desdemona's been seen in Othello's bed.

They tell me the pair are planning to wed!

BRABANTIO

She can't be with him. He was not born in Venice.

He may fight like a lion but in love he's a menace.

[Aside] Fathers will never get to grips with their daughters.

RODERIGO

Just follow me, sire. We'll head to his quarters.

SCENE II.

[IAGO is meeting with OTHELLO.]

IAGO
I should have killed Brabantio dead
For all the terrible things that he said.

OTHELLO
Sticks and stones may break my bones ...
He wants a marriage he condones.
I won her heart, I need his, not.

IAGO
Did you get married?

OTHELLO
     We tied the knot!
Our love is real, our love is pure.
And our legal status is secure.

IAGO
Brabantio will not like that.
You'd better grab your baseball bat!

OTHELLO
I appreciate the friendly warning.

Is that him there? God! What a morning!

[CASSIO appears.]

CASSIO
It's Cassio, sire. The Duke's in fear.
He's had bad news from Nicosia.
To Cyprus, he needs you now to go
To stop the Turks from running the show.

OTHELLO
Sounds like I'm the man for that.
I'll go and grab my fighting hat.

[OTHELLO exits.]

CASSIO
Now tell me, what are you're doing here?
Poisoning Othello's ear?

IAGO
How dare you, sir. We raised a glass.
The moor's just married Brabantio's lass.

[BRABANTIO and RODERIGO enter.]

Talk of the devil . . .

CASSIO
        and the devil appears

IAGO
[Drawing his sword] And there's Brabantio. I'll cut off his
    ears!

[Enter OTHELLO]

OTHELLO
[To IAGO] Hide your sword! *[To BRABANTIO]* Brabantio!
What's the meaning of this show?

BRABANTIO
I hear you've used your magic charms
To get my daughter in your arms.
You know I don't like refugees!
Roderigo, go and break his knees!

OTHELLO
If I had time, I'd fight you all.
But the Duke awaits me in his hall.
Cassio came to take me there.

BRABANTIO
Is that the truth?

IAGO
    It is. I swear!

BRABANTIO
We'll follow you the way you're heading
And beg the duke to annul your wedding!

OTHELLO
Saddle up, Brabantio,
Let's see which way the duke will go!

SCENE III.

The hall of the duke's palace

First Senator
By the look on this here Messenger's face,
I'd say the news isn't good, your Grace.

DUKE
He looks like he has seen a ghost!

Second Senator
Come over here and tell our host.

Messenger
To Cyprus now do sail the Turks
To rob the isle of all its perks.

Third Senator
That's just what we did not too long . . .

First Senator
[Interrupting] Ancient history, long and gone!

DUKE
How many boats? How many men?

Second Senator
They've got a lot.

Third Senator
You can say that again!
Ships alone there's one hundred and four.

Second Messenger
And they've stopped at Rhodes to pick up more!

First Senator
We need to send our bravest man.

Third Senator
If anyone can beat them, Othello can!

DUKE
Did you call the mighty Moor?

First Messenger
We did your grace; he's at the door.

DUKE
Well don't just stand there. Let him in!

[OTHELLO, IAGO, BRABANTIO, and CASSIO enter.]

Now there's a man who's born to win!
I guess you heard about our plight?
You must set sail this very night.
Brabantio, what are you doing here?

Third Senator
Have you come to volunteer?

BRABANTIO
Good lord, your Grace, that's quite absurd.

I've come to have an urgent word
About my daughter . . .

DUKE
> Is she dead?

BRABANTIO
No, no, my Lord she's gone and fled
Into a soldier's hairy arms.
Who must have used some magic charms
Cos the man she's with, to make it clear,
Is none other than Othello here!

OTHELLO
It is no magic trick, your Grace.
She fell in love with my handsome face.
I may not be the smoothest talker
But I'm good enough for this man's daughter!

BRABANTIO
You brought him here for another reason,
But stealing women here is treason!

OTHELLO
I stole her heart, that much is true.
But I didn't win her over you.
Your relationship will not go south.

DUKE
Let's hear it from the horse's mouth.

[DESDEMONA enters.]

DESDEMONA

I know that in Venice the law demands

A girl to follow her father's commands.

[Pointing at OTHELLO] But I've loved this man from the
very start

And have married him with my head and heart.

[to BRABANTIO] My mum she left her dad for you,

And now you must let me go too!

BRABANTIO

It looks as though I've failed you, child,

By being far too meek and mild

[Aside] A lesson here to take from me:

Keep your daughters under lock and key!

DUKE

Cheer up, old man, the bird has flown.

But with tears of grief you'll stay alone.

Just be a little more like me

And take your losses philosophically.

BRABANTIO

Like you have done with Cyprus?

DUKE

Oh don't be so ridiculous!

That's a loss of a different hue.

And the reason I sent for you [points to OTHELLO]

I know this is a passion killer

But you need to get hold of your tiller.

Hold off your matrimonial perks

And sail to beat those pesky Turks.

OTHELLO
As always, your Grace, I will do your bidding.

DESDEMONA
Sail off to war? You've got to be kidding!

DUKE
You can take her too, but please leave soon.

DESDEMONA
You promised me a honeymoon!

OTHELLO
You'll get one in Cyprus; that should be enough.
Good Iago will help you pack your stuff.

Second Senator
[To BRABANTIO] No kinder heart, no squarer jaw,
He'll make the perfect son-in-law.

DUKE
We'll leave you now, I'll rest my head.
I have a busy day ahead.
Good night, brave Moor, and Dessie too.

BRABANTIO
[to OTHELLO] She lied to me and she'll lie to you!

   [Exeunt BRABANTIO, DUKE, CASSIO, and the Senators.]

OTHELLO
You are the apple of my eye.
We have an hour before we fly.

So go with Iago and pack your kit.[9]
And join me in a little bit!

DESDEMONA
Well it's better than being left on the shelf . . .

[Exeunt OTHELLO and DESDEMONA]

RODERIGO
I'm going, too, to kill myself.
The girl I love is now his wife.

IAGO
But that's no reason to take your life.
That fighting man will give her the blues
So you must be prepared to jump in his shoes.
Believe me, my friend, we'll ruin that man.

RODERIGO
I'm a fool to trust you but I don't have a plan.

IAGO
Sell everything and take the cash.
To get that girl; we'll need a stash
And when she's yours. we'll all be elated
To see Othello humiliated.

RODERIGO
You alone shall guide my hand.
I'll leave right now to sell my land
And put together all the cash that I can.

---

9   British idiom for clothes.

IAGO

And tomorrow at my place, we'll continue the plan.

[Exit RODERIGO]

A fool and his money so easily parted.

That is the reason our 'friendship' got started.

That and to use him to ruin Othello.

Some say the Moor's a real charming fellow,

But he slept with my wife. Well, that is one notion.

But he certainly overlooked me for promotion.

I hate the bloke . . . but he likes me,

And when plotting revenge, that's the key!

I'll say his favourite, Cassio, looks

Like he's trying to get into Dessie's 'good books'.

Othello will believe me alright.

He has faith in me, which is such a delight.

With Cassio gone, I'll inherit his post,

And Othello's marriage will be as good as toast.

You are all my witnesses,

And now all my accomplices!

Act II

Scene I.

A cliff in Cyprus overlooking the sea

[MONTANO and two Gentlemen stare out to sea.]

MONTANO
A stormy sea, does it portend
Our final days in Cyprus, friend?

First Gentleman
I never saw the waves so mighty.

MONTANO
I did once, when I was in Blighty.[1]
But ships were in the harbour then,
Not out at sea and full of men.

[Second Gentleman enters.]

1　British idiom for Great Britain.

Second Gentleman
There are rumours flying all around
That the Turkish navy has been drowned.

MONTANO
And what about the Venetian boat
With Othello and Cassio? Do you know, does it float?

Second Gentleman
Well, Cassio's ship just arrived at the quay.[2]

First Gentleman
Is Othello with him?

MONTANO
    Let's go down and see!

[CASSIO enters.]

CASSIO
No need for that, Governor. I've come to see you.
I'm Othello's man, Cassio; how do you do?

First Gentleman
We're doing fine if the Turks are defeated.
But where is Othello? He deserves to be treated!

CASSIO
He hit the Turks from another ship
And with the swirling winds, he gave us the slip.

---

2 Pronounced "key"

MONTANO
I pray to God he'll be here soon.

CASSIO
He'll arrive, I'm sure, by late afternoon.

[A cannon is heard.]

Second Gentleman
The winds were foul, the sea was grim.

First Gentleman
Here's one more ship; maybe it's him?

[IAGO, DESDEMONA, RODERIGO, and EMILIA arrive.]

CASSIO
Desdemona . . . Othello's wife!
Thank the gods you're alive, I feared for your life.

IAGO
No need, good sir, she was under my care!

CASSIO
You look very healthy.

EMILIA
It's all the sea air.

[CASSIO kisses EMILIA and DESDEMONA.]

CASSIO
I hope you don't mind that I kissed you hello.

It's the custom round here.

EMILIA

    [Flattered] Well, what do you know!

IAGO

Not at all; Kiss away! It stops her from talking.
I've had twenty-four hours of her incessant squawking!

DESDEMONA

I won't hear you speak of your wife in that way.
Say something nice or have nothing to say!

IAGO

Then it's better to keep all my thoughts in my head.

DESDEMONA

Say something nice about me then instead.

CASSIO

Yes, come on Iago, while we wait for her man.
You can make her feel better.

IAGO

    No I can't.

EMILIA

    Yes you can!

IAGO

    [Aside, speaking of CASSIO who is comforting the ladies]

Keep holding their hands and giving them kisses.

Othello will hear more about you and his Mrs.
Whether it's true or whether its not!

[A trumpet sounds.]

And here he is now, let's move on my plot.

[OTHELLO enters.]

DESDEMONA
My love, my life, my man, Othello!
We arrived here half an hour ago.

OTHELLO
I don't know how you got here first,
But my love for you is fit to burst.
The Turks have drowned, the war is won.
Now we can have some honeymoon fun!

DESDEMONA
You were right. This is a lovely isle.

EMILIA
And they're bound to love your winning smile!

OTHELLO
Let's go and introduce you, dear.
Then finish up our nuptials here.

[Exeunt all but RODERIGO and IAGO]

RODERIGO
You see the way she looks at him?
She's filled with love up to the brim!

IAGO
What I see, dear Roderigo,
Is that she's in love with Cassio.

RODERIGO
With Cassio? Are you sure, my friend?

IAGO
Her marriage will soon be at an end.
Othello's old and lacking charms,
And Cassio, he has no qualms
About seduction of another's wife.

RODERIGO
With Othello's bride, he risks his life.
She will never break her vow.
She's far too moral anyhow!

IAGO
You didn't see their hands at play?
You've got to get him out of the way.
And you're standing here with a stupid frown!
You shouldn't take this lying down.

RODERIGO
Iago, please do all you can
To help me get rid of this man!

IAGO
Head down to the local inn

And wait 'til Cassio's filled his skin.[3]
Then shout some insult nice and loud
In front of locals in the crowd.
Cassio will not doubt kick your bum,
But when they see what he has done,
You'll get some local sympathy
And Cass will get thrown in the sea.

RODERIGO
And with Cassio gone, I'll be her first pick!
My clever friend, I'll get there quick.

[RODERIGO exits.]

IAGO
The Moor provides me with much humour.
He slept with my wife . . . Or was that just rumour?
But nevertheless, it's a good excuse
To go round handing out abuse.
Roderigo's a fool who'll just do as I ask.
So after he's finished his simplest of tasks,
I'll tell Othello of Cassio's woos,
And sit back and enjoy all the trouble that brews.

---

3   A reference to the idiom "had a skinful", meaning to get drunk.

SCENE II.

A square in the city

Herald
Oh yay, oh yay, I bring you perks!
Othello has finished off the Turks.
He's arranged for us a bit of a do,
Which is what I'm out here announcing to you.
He also got married, which we'll all celebrate
In this town hall square from five until late.
Go put on your frocks and shine your medallions,
And God bless the Moor and all the Italians!

SCENE III.

In the castle

[OTHELLO, DESDEMONA, and CASSIO enter.]

CASSIO
Does the party please you, sir?

OTHELLO
Oh yes it does,

DESDEMONA
    and I concur.
Now can we go to bed, my dear?

OTHELLO
[To CASSIO] Don't let the men drink all the beer!

CASSIO
Iago's in charge; what could go wrong?

OTHELLO
You keep an eye too. We'll be running along.

*[OTHELLO and DESDEMONA exit. IAGO
enters, a little drunk.]*

CASSIO
Good Iago, you're here. Looking after the men?

IAGO
A bit early for that. It's not even ten.

CASSIO
Othello's in bed.

IAGO
Well, no surprise there.
His wife's pretty fit.

CASSIO
She's certainly fair.

IAGO
I know you think she's sexy and sassy.

CASSIO
I'd rather describe her as cultured and classy.

IAGO
I think you need to loosen up.
I've got some wine; go grab a cup.

CASSIO
I've had one already and I am no fool.
One glass per day is my personal rule.

IAGO
Oh come on, Cass. The lads are outside.
You've got to drink more or you'll damage my pride.

CASSIO

I've seen the harm that drinking can do!

IAGO

Don't worry, I'm sure it won't happen to you.

Now go and let my buddy in.

He's brought some whisky, wine, and gin

[CASSIO exits.]

Another drink and he will be

Looking to fight and perfect for me.

I made sure Roderigo he knows what to do.

[CASSIO enters finishing a drink.]

And Cassio's back, rather drunk, right on cue!

[RODERIGO and MONTANO enter.]

CASSIO

I've drunk too much.

MONTANO

    No more than a glass.

CASSIO

If you don't hold me up, I'll fall flat on my ass.

IAGO

[Singing]

The soldier he does like a drink, so give us all a beer.

And clink our glasses loudly, and we will have good cheer.

CASSIO
What a wonderful song and sung with such vim.
Let's wake up the General and sing it for him!

IAGO
Not sure if that's the wisest thing.

CASSIO
You think that I am drunk? Stop talking and sing.
No, wait a second; I've got something to do.
Can someone point me the way to the loo?

[CASSIO exits.]

IAGO
It's a shame when a man is a slave to the drink.

MONTANO
Is he often like this?

IAGO
    Well what do you think?

MONTANO
I think that a man who likes a nip
Ought not keep his lieutenantship.

[RODERIGO enters.]

IAGO
We were just saying, Rodders, that Cassio looked grim.
[Knowingly] If I were you, I'd follow him . . .

[RODERIGO exits.]

MONTANO
I feel that we should tell his boss.

IAGO
We shouldn't, my friend. It would just make him cross,
And Cassio is a friend of mine
Who I'd rather help through this difficult time.

*[Shouts from off of "Help! Help!" RODERIGO runs in injured,
pursued by CASSIO.]*

CASSIO
Come back here and finish this brawl.
I'll kick your arse to Limassol.[4]

MONTANO
Lieutenant, what on earth is wrong?

CASSIO
This man, good sir, did try it on.[5]
He said that I was drunk and loud
And upsetting all the Cypriot crowd.

[He hits RODERIGO, who whimpers.]

MONTANO
.He's got a point. Now hush your cries.

---

4   A city in Cyprus

5   British idiom for doing something to deliberately anger or annoy someone

[*Pushing RODERIGO out of the way*] And stand and fight a
  man your size

[*MONTANO and CASSIO begin fighting.*]

IAGO
[*Aside to RODERIGO*] Well don't just stand there keeping
  quiet.
Go and shout that there's a riot.

[*RODERIGO exits.*]

Gentlemen, stop! God help us all!
I hate to see two soldiers maul!

[*A bell tolls.*]

And who is that who rings the alarm?
We're supposed to keep this island calm.

[*OTHELLO enters.*]

OTHELLO
Stop fighting here. What's this I see?
Stop this at once

MONTANO
[*In a headlock*] He's hurting me.

IAGO
The General's here; lay down your swords.

OTHELLO
You're acting like the Turkish hordes.
We came to stop a killing spree,

Not start one of our own . . . who's he?

IAGO
It's Cassio, sir.

OTHELLO
    [To CASSIO] Have you lost your mind?

IAGO
He's normally not the brawling kind.

CASSIO
[Suffering] I have no words . . .

OTHELLO
    Then speak no more.
Montano, what were you fighting for?
You're famously both mild and meek.

MONTANO
[Exhausted] Ask Iago; I cannot speak.

OTHELLO
If someone doesn't spill the beans,
I'll blame you all, and you know what that means . . .

MONTANO
[Aside to IAGO] You may be loyal to Cassio, sir,
But you must tell him what did occur.

IAGO
[To OTHELLO] I'd rather die than rat on Cass,
But I'll tell you the truth about what came to pass:

Montano and I were shooting the breeze
When a man ran in crying for help, if you please.
Cassio was chasing him,
And that is when Montano stepped in.
I followed the man that Cassio chased,
But he gave me the slip so I came back in haste.
And when I returned these two were fighting
With Cassio out of control.

MONTANO

He was frightening!

IAGO

But show him some mercy, my Lord, if you can.
He's normally such a sensible man.

OTHELLO

Loyal Iago, fair as ever,
You're defending this man who has acted in error.
Cassio's deeds have brought shame on our nation.
[To CASSIO] You are stripped of your rank and your good
    reputation.

[Enter DESDEMONA]

DESDEMONA

Othello, my dear, I woke up and you'd gone.
What's happening here?

OTHELLO

There's a fight going on.
But it's over now! We can go back to bed.

Montano, my doctors will take care of your head.

[All exeunt apart from IAGO and CASSIO.]

IAGO
Are you injured, my friend? You took some big blows.

CASSIO
Well only my ego, as far as it goes.
I've lost it all by being weak.
My reputation's up the creek!

IAGO
The fellow you chased, what had he said?

CASSIO
I can't now remember; I'd be better off dead!

IAGO
Don't talk that way. That is nonsense, my friend.
Othello was cross but with time he will mend.
In the morning, go find him and plead for your case!

CASSIO
I'm far too embarrassed to meet face-to-face,
And hungover, and angry! Oh why did I drink?!

IAGO
Go see Desdemona. She will help you, I think.
Her husband respects her and I know she likes you.
If she pleads for your case, I'm sure he'll come through.

CASSIO

That's good advice; you're wise and kind.

Maybe she can change his mind.

I'll go to bed now, noble sir.

Tomorrow I will visit her.

[Exit CASSIO]

IAGO

That really is such 'good advice'.

Othello's bride is just so 'nice'.

And as she listens to Cassio's fears,

I'll go and bend her husband's ears.

I'll say that his wife, whom he does trust,

Harbours now a shameless lust.

So the more she pleads young Cassio's case,

The more he'll see her treacherous face.

Like a fly that's caught in a spider's net,

The more she pleads, the more jealous he'll get.

[Enter RODERIGO, with luggage]

Roderigo, my friend.

RODERIGO

    Don't you 'friend' me, you menace.

I'm broken and beaten and leaving for Venice.

IAGO

At a time like this? Why so morose?

Can't you see that we are close?

Tonight we got Cassio out of the way.

A little discomfort is a small price to pay!
Our plan will prevail. Trust me and stay!
Othello's demise is hours away!

RODERIGO
Why do I do what you always insist?

[Exit RODERIGO from whence he came]

IAGO
Because I am the devil; you just can't resist.
And as dawn it breaks, my darling bride
Will help persuade Dessy to take Cassio's side.
And the moment she does, I'll bring in her man.
He'll see them together. It's a brilliant plan!

Act III

SCENE I.

In the castle.

[CASSIO alone. Enter IAGO.]

IAGO
[Aside] The morning after the night before.
What joys do you think today has in store?

CASSIO
Iago, my nearest and dearest of friends,
I'm here for Othello to make my amends.
Last night was probably the worst of my life.
So first, I want a chat with your wife.
I want her to set up a meeting for me
With Desdemona personally.

IAGO
A splendid idea, I'll see if she can.

[IAGO exits.]

CASSIO
What a kind and saintly man.

[EMILIA enters.]

What a coincidence. And right on cue.

EMILIA
Othello and Des are talking about you.
Desdemona says that you shouldn't have been sacked,
But her husband suggests that the man you attacked
Is a bigwig around here, so you must pay some price.
But then he'll forgive you. Now isn't that nice?

CASSIO
So Desdemona is pleading my case?
Do you think I could thank her? Alone? Face-to-face?

EMILIA
Come in with me. She'd like that too.
At the end of the day, what harm could it do?

[EMILIA and CASSIO exeunt.]

CENE II

At the quay

[Enter OTHELLO and IAGO.]

OTHELLO
Find my ship's captain on one of his boats,
And tell him, 'Deliver to Venice these notes
To the Senate from their favourite son'.
Now I'll walk to the fort. Meet me there when you're
    done.

IAGO
I will, my lord, after delivering your parcel,
Come up and join you there at the castle.

[OTHELLO and IAGO exeunt in different directions.]

SCENE III.

The castle

[DESDEMONA, EMILIA, and CASSIO enter.]

DESDEMONA
Cassio, I will plead your case.

EMILIA
For my husband's sake, your Grace.
You'd think this problem was his own.

DESDEMONA
I'll say again you're not alone.

CASSIO
Your empathy's not typical.

DESDEMONA
His decision was political.
Trust me, dear, he likes you a lot.

CASSIO
But without my job, I'll be forgot.

DESDEMONA
Forget you sir? There is no way.
I'll pester him both night and day.

EMILIA
He loves you so he'll listen to you.

DESDEMONA
It's the very least that I can do.
I'd rather drink from a poison cup
Than have my husband give you up!

[IAGO and OTHELLO enter.]

EMILIA
Your husband, ma'am, does this way walk.

CASSIO
I'll leave you then . . .

DESDEMONA
    No. Stay and talk.

CASSIO
I don't think that the timing's right.

DESDEMONA
Very well. I'll say good night.

[CASSIO exits.]

IAGO
I like that not . . .

OTHELLO
    What did you say?
Did you see Cassio stealing away?

IAGO
There's not a chance that Cassio might
Be visiting Des at this time of the night!

DESDEMONA
My husband! What a timely call.
Did you see Cassio in the hall?
He came to plead his case to me
So you would treat him favourably.
He came here all 'alas and alack'.
Tell me, will you take him back?

OTHELLO
That was him in here just then?

DESDEMONA
Shall I call him back again?

OTHELLO
Not right now, some other day!

DESDEMONA
Oh tell me when. You have to say.
His actions were a mystery,
But we three have such history.
Remember when my love you did want?
We both called him our 'confidant'.
Let me call him back again.

OTHELLO
Not now. Perhaps later. Don't ask again!

DESDEMONA
But if not now, then tell me when.
Tomorrow? Tuesday? Wednesday night?

OTHELLO
Whenever you want. Just shut up, alright?

DESDEMONA
Don't act as though you do it for me.
It's hardly a great difficulty.

OTHELLO
Anything. Please just get out of here.

DESDEMONA
As you demand, I obey, my dear.

[DESDEMONA and EMILIA exit.]

OTHELLO
I never loved a girl so well.
If I did not, I'd go to hell.

IAGO
So you both knew Cassio before these days?

OTHELLO
He helped us through our courting phase.
He often delivered notes for us.

IAGO
Oh really?

OTHELLO

Yes. Now what's the fuss?

Do you think he is an honest fellow?

IAGO

'Honest', you say? Well, as far as I know.

OTHELLO

But what do you think? What do you see?

IAGO

What do I think?

OTHELLO

Stop mimicking me!

Your brow is creased, your eyes are too.

Now tell me what is troubling you!

IAGO

I beg you, sir, most humbly,

Please do not ask that of me.

Cassio's honest; of that I'm sure.

It's just my thoughts that are impure.

OTHELLO

You honest men are scared to spout

What evil men do shout about!

IAGO

I say with caution and with care,

Beware the green-eyed monster's stare.

If you worship your wife, yet doubt her too.

That ogre will come looking for you.

A poor man is rich if content with his lot,
But a rich man is poor if he thinks he is not.

OTHELLO
To this monster's glare I am not bound.
Even if such proof you found,
And did to me some evidence show,
Both love and jealousy I'd let go.
My love is strong and my sense not weak.

IAGO
Reassured, my lord, I'll freely speak.
You trust too much. You should suspect.
From Cassio, sir, you should protect
Yourself and your young nubile bride.
They could combine to hurt your pride.
She deceived her father, did she not,
To get the husband she has got?

OTHELLO
She did indeed; I'm in your debt.
But Desdemona I trust yet.

IAGO
I'm sorry, General, my mind is lewd
And now I fear I've spoiled the mood.

OTHELLO
There's no need to apologize.
You've just helped me to open my eyes.
Off you go and ask your missus
To look out for some funny business.

IAGO
I will, good sir.

[IAGO exits.]

OTHELLO
    I trust too much.
That's who I am and so as such,
I'm vulnerable to low deceit.
But with Iago's help, this curse I'll beat.
He knows more than he tells, I see.
And I have to say, that bothers me!

[Enter IAGO]

IAGO
An idea came to me just when I'd gone;
Take Cassio back like a prodigal son.
But not just yet. Let's make him wait.
Take him at some future date.
And if your wife shows reservations,
Perhaps my fears have some foundations.

[Exit IAGO]

OTHELLO
It could turn out that Iago's my saviour.
He knows so much about human behaviour.
So kind and brave to tell me his fear.
If she is cheating on me, she'll be out on her ear.
It is true that the wives of powerful men
More often are unfaithful to them.

To cheat on me, of course, she could
But I still cannot believe she would!

[Enter DESDEMONA and EMILIA]

DESDEMONA
My darling, are you feeling ill?
The Cypriot lords are waiting still.

OTHELLO
I cannot eat; My head it aches.

DESDEMONA
A little love is all it takes.
This handkerchief will soothe your pain.

[DESDEMONA tries to wrap her handkerchief around
OTHELLO's head, but it is too small.]

OTHELLO
It's far too small; don't try again.

[The handkerchief falls to the floor.]

Just walk with me, come take my arm.
[Taking DESDEMONA's arm] This, I know, my head will
calm.

[OTHELLO and DESDEMONA exit.]

EMILIA

[Finding the handkerchief and picking it up]

I can't believe she left this here,

A present from her husband dear.
When spying on her, I've seen her kiss it.
Before too long she's bound to miss it.
My husband longs for this little thing.
I will copy its pattern, then give it to him.

[Enter IAGO]

IAGO
Alone again? Well, there's a surprise!

EMILIA
Less of the cheek, and open your eyes;
I picked up Dessie's handkerchief.

IAGO
You stole it from her?

EMILIA
            I am no thief!
She dropped it here by accident.

IAGO
And you picked it up.

EMILIA
            Just after they went.
I don't know why you want it so.

IAGO
Just give it to me. *[A small struggle]* Let it go!

EMILIA
[Giving it up] I hope your plans are honourable.
My lady's very vulnerable.
She needs that when she's on her own.

IAGO
Oh mind your business and leave me alone.

[EMILIA exits.]

I'll leave it at Cassio's for him to discover.
An inconsequent thing doesn't mean he's her lover.
But the general's mind is full of doubt.
Who knows what he'll think when he finds out?

[OTHELLO enters.]

[Knowingly] I take it, sir, you didn't sleep well?

OTHELLO
No I did not; you go to hell.
My restful sleep you took from me.
My mind it plays such trickery.
I'm cursed to doubt and not to know.
If you have proof, then let it show,
Unless you've cursed my mind for sport,
In which case I shall spare you nought.
You'll wish that you had killed my Des;
The punishment would hurt you less!

IAGO
I did not mean to be unkind.
I only meant to speak my mind.

But now I see that was a mistake.

From here on in my thoughts I'll take,

And bury them, lest they offend.

OTHELLO

You'd better watch your step, my friend!

Can I really believe my wife is not true?

[Referring to Iago and Desdemona] How can I trust either of
    you?

I swing like some cursed pendulum.

If you have proof, pray give me some.

You have something substantial?

IAGO

Only circumstantial.

Cassio wiped his beard today

In, how should I say, an effeminate way?

He used a hanky small and cute.

On it were embroidered fruit,

Strawberries I think they were.

OTHELLO

[Shocked, dropping to his knees]

That's the one I gave to her.

I swear to God I'll take his life.

IAGO

I'll help you sir, but spare your wife.

OTHELLO

I'll think about how to punish the whore,

But Cassio he shall live no more.

IAGO
Cassio will die, just tell me how.

OTHELLO
Within three days, promise it now!

IAGO
Whatever it takes, I know I can.

OTHELLO
Then follow me, my loyal man.

SCENE IV.

Desdemona's room

[Enter DESDEMONA and EMILIA]

DESDEMONA
I must have left it somewhere near.

EMILIA
You always keep it very dear.

DESDEMONA
It's a keepsake from Othello.

EMILIA
Is your man a jealous fellow?

DESDEMONA
Luckily not, I'm happy to say.

EMILIA
Other men might suspect foul play!

DESDEMONA
Not my husband, not with me.

EMILIA
And here he comes.

DESDEMONA

Just watch, you'll see.

[Enter OTHELLO]

My love, did you yet find the time
To take care of that favour of mine?

OTHELLO

Before you start to give me grief
Let me have your handkerchief.
I have a cold.

DESDEMONA

[Giving OTHELLO another handkerchief] Perhaps the
flu?

OTHELLO

Where's the one that I gave to you?

DESDEMONA

The one with the embroidered stitch?

OTHELLO

Made with magic by a powerful witch,
The fruits were coloured with virgin hearts.
The magic silk affects the parts
Of the body that a loving husband gives
To his faithful wife as long as she lives.

DESDEMONA

It's as precious as that? I wish that you'd said.

OTHELLO
Mum gave it to me when on her deathbed.
It's worth more to me than any jewel
And you've lost it?

DESDEMONA
      No! I am not such a fool.
It's just misplaced. And why this act?
From Cassio's plight do you distract?

OTHELLO
Make good your loss!

DESDEMONA
      Take Cassio back!

OTHELLO
[Threateningly] I am your boss!

DESDEMONA
      Stop your attack!

OTHELLO
I'll stop it when you show to me
Your handkerchief and . . . fidelity!

               [OTHELLO exits.]

EMILIA
You were lucky that you were not harmed.

DESDEMONA
That handkerchief must indeed be charmed.

EMILIA
Not jealous, you said? Am I right my friend?
All men do act that way in the end.

[Enter CASSIO and IAGO]

IAGO
Only she can change his view.
[Noticing DESDEMONA] And there she is. Oh lucky you!

CASSIO
I see that you are feeling grim,
But did you get to speak to him?
Just to know what is my fate?

DESDEMONA
He's very angry. You'll have to wait.

CASSIO
Very angry?

IAGO
        Am I delirious?
He's never angry! It must be serious!
Shall I go and have a word?

DESDEMONA
Yes, go and find out what's occurred.

[IAGO exits.]

The handkerchief was just a trigger,
A sign of something much, much bigger.
I give that man no cause for doubt.

EMILIA
A monster in him grows without
Good reason.

DESDEMONA
    Let it grow no more.

EMILIA
You need to do something, to be sure.

DESDEMONA
I'll go to my husband.

CASSIO
    I hope you do!

DESDEMONA
And once he's calmed down, I'll ask about you.

       [DESDEMONA and EMILIA exeunt.]

       [BIANCA enters.]

BIANCA
My love! At last. Where on earth have you been?
It's been seven days and nights since I've seen
And felt your body on me.

CASSIO
    . . . Yes I know.
There's a lot going on; I've been feeling quite low.
I'll come and see you soon, you'll see.
But before then, copy this hanky for me.

BIANCA
This is fine and it's fancy. Where was it found?

CASSIO
In my room, don't know how, just there on the ground.

BIANCA
Is this the reason I've not had a call?

CASSIO
Oh, don't start being jealous; it's nothing at all!

BIANCO
Well something this nice is bound to be missed.

CASSIO
So copy it please.

BIANCA
    If you really insist.

CASSIO
And it's not that I don't love you, my dear,
But leave me to meet my general here.
I don't want him to see me with you.

BIANCA
I know you don't love me, but what can I do?
Just promise me to visit tonight.

CASSIO
I promise you that. Now please go.

BIANCA

Yes, alright.

[They exeunt.]

Act IV

Scene I.

In the Castle

[Enter IAGO and OTHELLO]

OTHELLO
Do you think they have kissed? Or done something
more?

IAGO
If she just gave one kiss, it's best to ignore.

OTHELLO
Just one mistake doesn't make her impure.

IAGO
But that handkerchief, sir?

OTHELLO
He has got that, I'm sure.

IAGO
If he has, then he has her honour as well.

OTHELLO
Damn that man and that woman, I curse them to hell.

[OTHELLO faints and starts having a fit.]

IAGO
[Aside] It's the green-eyed beast that eats him, of course,
And his innocent wife will feel its full force.

[CASSIO enters.]

CASSIO
What's happening to him?

IAGO
    Epileptic fit.
But it's short, he's coming out of it!

CASSIO
Yes. Look. I think he's coming round.

IAGO
Then you should really go to ground.
We'll speak again soon.

[CASSIO exits.]

    My Lord, you're awake!

OTHELLO
Help me up, for goodness' sake.

IAGO

She's not the first unfaithful wife,

So be a man and bear this strife.

When you were knocked out, Cassio came.

I made some excuse but he'll be back again.

OTHELLO

Did he confess?

IAGO

No he did not,

But on his return, he'll tell me the lot.

So hide over there; you'll hear his confession,

But act like a man and control your aggression.

[OTHELLO hides.]

[Aside] As he looks on with wrath and rancour,

I'll quiz Cassio about Bianca,

The prostitute who does adore

The young lieutenant. But the whore

He keeps just to amuse

And she seems content with his abuse.

[CASSIO enters.]

You're back, Lieutenant.

CASSIO

I've lost my commission!

IAGO

Just keep asking Dessie to beg your remission.

[Pause] Imagine if Bianca could promote you somehow?

CASSIO
If she could do that, I'd be a general by now!

[He laughs.]

OTHELLO
[From his hiding place] He laughs at my fate.

CASSIO
    She loves me, poor thing.
She wants to get married.

IAGO
    Then buy her a ring!

[CASSIO is laughing.]

OTHELLO
The winner gets the final laugh.

CASSIO
She's spreading rumours that are not true by half.

[IAGO signals to OTHELLO to come closer.]

OTHELLO
He beckons me closer to Cassio's voice.

CASSIO
She's doting on me; I don't have a choice!
She hangs on my neck until it is red.
[Miming and laughing] Then starts shaking my body.

OTHELLO
That's those two in bed!

IAGO
And here she is.

BIANCA
A word with you.

CASSIO
Have you got nothing better to do?

BIANCA
I'm bringing your hanky back, you see?
Don't pass your lover's gifts to me.
If I take it from you, I'm a whore and a thief.

OTHELLO
That's my bloody handkerchief!

BIANCA
If you want me later, you know where I am.

[BIANCA exits.]

IAGO
If I were you, I'd follow her, man.

CASSIO
I think I should or she'll shout through the streets.

IAGO
I'll meet you there later, once you've been in her sheets.

CASSIO
Don't let me down Iago; I fear for my plight.

IAGO
Just leave it with me. See you after midnight!

> *[CASSIO exits. OTHELLO appears.]*

OTHELLO
In which way shall I murder the cur?

IAGO
Did you see him laugh about sleeping with her?
And the handkerchief?

OTHELLO
 It was mine? You are sure?

IAGO
She gave it to him and he to his whore.
That's the disdain that he has for your bride,
And such brazen cheek. He could at least try to hide!

OTHELLO
[About Desdemona] Such a delicate flower. Her grace stood
  alone.
She melted my heart. Now she's turned it to stone.
So much beauty and talent the world's yet to see.
How could she go and do this to me?

IAGO
And with your Lieutenant.

OTHELLO

She betrayed her prince.
I'll kill her with poison.

IAGO

I'll try to convince
You not to do that. Strangle her instead!
And what's more poetic than in her own bed?

OTHELLO

Excellent. Good. I will do the deed.

IAGO

And I will kill Cassio.

OTHELLO

Then we are agreed.
I'll take care of her and you of that menace.

[A trumpet sounds.]

Hear ye the trumpet?

IAGO

It's someone from Venice.
Lodovico's coming. A note from the duke?
And Dessie's with him.

OTHELLO

I'm going to puke!

[Enter LODOVICO, DESDEMONA, and Attendants.]

Greetings, Sir

LODOVICO

This letter's for you.

It's a note from the duke saying what you should do.

DESDEMONA

Welcome, cousin Lodovico.

IAGO

Welcome to Cyprus.

LODOVICO

How does it go?

We hear the island it does thrive.

And how is Cassio?

IAGO

Well . . . he is alive.

DESDEMONA

My husband and he had a bit of a row.[6]

But I'm sure you can sort it out somehow.

In my heart, for Cassio, much care I find.

OTHELLO

What did you say? Are you out of your mind?

DESDEMONA

Why are you angry? You are never like this.

LODOVICO

Maybe the letter gives him reason to diss?

The duke wants him home and Cassio here.

---

6   British term for fight or argument, rhymes with "now".

DESDEMONA
I'm happy for him.

OTHELLO
Are you really, my dear?

DESDEMONA
Yes I am.

OTHELLO
You admit it? In public as well?

DESDEMONA
I don't see the problem.

OTHELLO
You're as guilty as hell!

[He strikes DESDEMONA.]

DESDEMONA
I swear I've done nothing.

LODOVICO
What did I just see?
She's crying, Othello!

OTHELLO
That means nothing to me!
You can cry there for years; I will never believe.
That you're sad. Get you gone!

LODOVICO

She would never deceive...

OTHELLO

What is it that you want with her?

You want her to stay? Is that it, good sir?

To hear her fake, unfaithful cries

And listen to her gruesome lies?

Away you witch, perform elsewhere.

In time I'll come and find you there.

[DESDEMONA exits.]

I will obey the duke's commands.

Cassio will replace me as his lordship demands.

Tonight we'll drink and stuff our throats.

Welcome to Cyprus, monkeys and goats!

[OTHELLO exits.]

LODOVICO

I can't believe what I have seen.

He struck his wife! He was never that mean!

This was a man without any flaws,

Who never got angry, no matter the cause.

IAGO

Cyprus has changed him.

LODOVICO

Is he losing his mind?

IAGO

To say something like that, sir, is very unkind.

LODOVICO
But to hit his own wife!

IAGO
That's true. It's not nice.

LODOVICO
Has he done it before?

IAGO
One could say once or twice.
But I wouldn't, of course. I'm far too loyal.
And a man's reputation I am not one to spoil.
You will judge for yourself the extent of his ways.

LODOVICO
No doubt I will in the forthcoming days.

$\mathcal{S}$CENE II·

In Desdemona's room

[OTHELLO and EMILIA enter.]

OTHELLO
So you're telling me she's done no wrong?

EMILIA
She's honest as the day is long.

OTHELLO
Did you see her flirt with Cassio?

EMILIA
If she did, to hell I'll go!
I cannot guess where you got the idea.
Some evil force has bent your ear.
I will tell you again even though you resist,
A more honest wife just does not exist.

OTHELLO
Go bring this 'honest' wife to me.

        [EMILIA exits.]

The woman speaks dishonestly.
It's one of the brothel owner's chores

To lie through her teeth to protect her whores.

[DESDEMONA and EMILIA enter.]

Come hither, woman, let me see.

DESDEMONA
What horror do you see in me?

OTHELLO
[to EMILIA] Leave us now to what comes out.
And if somebody approaches, give us a shout!

[EMILIA exits.]

DESDEMONA
Of course. I see you're furious
But know not why.

OTHELLO
    Are you curious?

DESDEMONA
I will always want to know your mind.
I am your wife; I'm true and kind

OTHELLO
Go ahead, lie to my face,
You cheating whore . . .

DESDEMONA
    Enough, your grace!
You think I am a courtesan?

OTHELLO
All other sins I know I can
Face with the patience of Job.
But your harlot's act does take my robe
Of dignity and self-respect.
What future can I now expect?
You've robbed me of my dignity.

DESDEMONA
And what have you, sir, robbed from me?
I gave myself only to you.

OTHELLO
You're telling me it isn't true?
You're not a whore?

DESDEMONA
        I swear to thee.

OTHELLO
I mistake then your identity.
A Venetian girl I took you for
That stole the heart of this innocent Moor.
[Calling to EMILIA offstage] Madam, here's the fee I owe

[EMILIA enters.]

For spending time here with your ho!

[OTHELLO exits.]

EMILIA
Are you alright? What are his fears?

DESDEMONA

My only answer is my tears.

Put fresh sheets on my bed, my dear.

Then go and fetch your husband here.

[EMILIA exits.]

Did I not until recently

Treat my husband decently?

What spirit overcomes my man?

[Enter IAGO and EMILIA.]

IAGO

Iago at your service, ma'am.

Tell me now what has occurred.

EMILIA

You won't believe a single word.

Her husband he just yelled, and swore,

And accused his wife of being a whore.

DESDEMONA

Iago, is it true that I...

EMILIA

Of course not, dear. Try not to cry.

[of DESDEMONA] She's shocked of course and full of fear.

IAGO

From whence did he get this idea?

EMILIA

This smells of someone's twisted game

To put this innocent in the frame,
Some social-climbing, evil fool.

IAGO
Surely no one is that cruel.

EMILIA
It smacks of the same trickery
That convinced you the Moor had slept with me!

IAGO
Oh shut your mouth . . .

EMILIA
    Is it a trick?
Some villain's scheme to make Othello sick?
If I did catch who told this lie,
His life I'd take.

DESDEMONA
    Iago, why
Does he abuse me so?
Only to him my love I show.
Loyal Iago, you know his mind.
Why is he being so unkind?

IAGO
Let me help allay your fear.
Othello's worried about his career.
In times of stress we all can be
Extremely cruel. Yes, even me!

DESDEMONA
I hope that's all it is, dear friend.

IAGO
I'm sure we'll find a happy end.

[Trumpets sound.]

Now dry your eyes; you're not a sinner.
Go through and show your face at dinner.

[Exeunt DESDEMONA and EMILIA]

[Enter RODERIGO]

Here he is, my favourite chap.

RODERIGO
Iago, please just cut the crap.
I've done most everything you said
And I'm nowhere nearer Dessie's bed.
I'm further away than when we met.

IAGO
Oh that's not true.

RODERIGO
    You wanna bet?
Not only that, I'm stony broke.
I've nothing left.

IAGO
    Poor thing!

RODERIGO
You joke?
The jewels I gave you to have some fun
Should have me sleeping with a nun!
You told me that she liked them all,
And still there is no booty-call.
I'm done with you!

IAGO
I'm not your owner!

RODERIGO
I'm going now to Desdemona.
To try and get my jewels back!

IAGO
And if you don't?

RODERIGO
Then I'll attack!
You'll feel the force of my frustration.

IAGO
You've risen in my estimation!
You're right to be annoyed with me!
My long-term plan is hard to see.
But now I see you have the powers
To wait another twenty-four hours.
If she is not your girl by then,
We will stand this way again,
And you may do whatever you can.

RODERIGO
I take it then you have a plan?
Tell me if it's reasonable.

IAGO
I think you'll find it feasible.
Cassio here now runs the show.

RODERIGO
That's news to me!

IAGO
     He's yet to know!

RODERIGO
So Othello and Des will go away?

IAGO
They will, unless we make them stay;
Cassio we will kill tonight.
Then all our plans will turn out right.
Between the hours of twelve and one,
He'll visit his whore to have some fun.
Just grab him near the water trough.
Then I'll jump out and we'll finish him off.

RODERIGO
We'll punish him for which of his crimes?

IAGO
After what I tell you, you will kill him three times.
But the night draws near, we must make haste.

RODERIGO
Indeed, we have no time to waste.

[Exit IAGO and RODERIGO]

SCENE III.

In the castle

[Enter DESDEMONA, EMILIA, LODOVICO, and OTHELLO.]

OTHELLO
Lodovico, can we walk?

LODOVICO
There is no need.

OTHELLO
    I want to talk.
The evening air has cleared my head.
Desdemona, go to bed!
Do not have your maid stay there with thee,
And I will join you presently.

        [Exeunt OTHELLO and LODOVICO]

EMILIA
He seems a lot calmer; what did he say?

DESDEMONA
He said, 'Go to bed', and to send you away.
So pass me my nightgown and get off home.
I need to face my husband alone.

EMILIA
The wedding sheets I put on the bed.

DESDEMONA
You'll wrap me in them if you find me there dead.

EMILIA
Your man you think could kill his wife?

DESDEMONA
And yet I'll love him all my life.
My mother's maid did have a ditty.
She too was abused; it's a terrible pity.
She sang it as she passed away,
And that song has been in my head all day.

EMILIA
Shall I fetch your night dress, dear?

DESDEMONA
No need; my husband's probably near.
[Pause] Lodovico is handsome, is he not?
He speaks very well.

EMILIA
    I think that he's hot.

DESDEMONA
[Singing]
    The poor soul sat sighing by a sycamore tree,
    Her hand on her bosom, her head on her knee.
    The fresh streams ran by her and murmured her
        moans.

Her salt tears fell from her and softened the stones.

Prithee, my husband will come here anon—

And a wreath made of willow is what I'll put on.

Let nobody blame him, his scorn I approve—

That's not how it goes.

[Hearing something outside] Did something there move?

EMILIA
Only the wind

DESDEMONA
I hope so, my friend.

EMILIA
I'd better go now.

DESDEMONA
I've remembered the end.
[Singing]

I called my love false, but what said he then?

If I court more women, you'll couch more men.

My eyes are itchy, I'll be crying tonight.

EMILIA
That's just an old wives' tale. I'm sure that's not right.

DESDEMONA
You really think wives do cheat on their men?

EMILIA
I'm sure that some do . . .

DESDEMONA

Would you do it then?
For the world, I would not ...

EMILIA

The world's a big prize
For one little sin.

DESDEMONA

Well not in my eyes.

EMILIA

If we cheat on our husbands, the man is to blame.
If he sleeps with another and puts us to shame,
Or acts over-jealous or we're beaten, like you,
Or cuts our allowance, what else should we do?
They choose to give in to their carnal desire
So why shouldn't we do what they inspire?
If they abuse us, here's one little gem
To act in the way that we've learned from them.

DESDEMONA

Emilia, I'll tell you flat,
I wish to learn from women like that.
Not to follow their lead but to avoid their plight.
And with that, good lady, I will bid you goodnight.

Act V

SCENE I.

In the street of Bianca's house

[IAGO and RODERIGO enter.]

IAGO
Right. Here we are. I will stand guard.
And when you hit him, hit him hard.
This act right here will us make or break.
So get it right for goodness' sake.

RODERIGO
Please stay close.

IAGO
    I'll be right here.
He's just a man, no need to fear.

RODERIGO
I can't say that I like this stuff,

But he has given me reason enough.

IAGO
[Aside] Who kills who, it's the same for me.
But I'd like to keep Rod's jewellery!
So Cassio I'll root for him!
No, that is but a foolish whim.
His smoothness makes us all seem rough
And of his beauty I've seen enough.
He knows the truth to all my lies.
Here's the place where Cassio dies!

RODERIGO

[CASSIO enters.]

I hear him come. Just one more stride.
[Calling] Prepare to die, don't try to hide.

[Stabbing CASSIO]

CASSIO

[Uninjured, drawing his sword]

You common villain, cowardly thief,
I wear my armour underneath.
And now you'll feel my blade instead.
Take that you cad!

[CASSIO stabs RODERIGO.]

RODERIGO
I think I'm dead.

[IAGO approaches CASSIO from behind, slices his sword through CASSIO's leg, and exits unseen.]

CASSIO
I'm cut right through. You've crippled my leg.

RODERIGO
What a villain I am.

CASSIO
   Someone help me, I beg.

[OTHELLO enters unseen.]

OTHELLO
Iago he has kept his word.

CASSIO
[Calling] Is someone there? Have I been heard?

OTHELLO
[To himself] You have indeed, *[About Iago]* Oh trusted
   friend,
You've brought his foul life to an end.
Iago shows his love for me,
His most devoted loyalty.
[About DESDEMONA] Your lover's dead, he goes to hell!
And soon you will go there as well.
You've stained our sheets with acts of lust,
And now with blood. My word you trust!

[OTHELLO exits.]

[LODOVICO and GRATIANO enter.]

CASSIO
Help me please. Is anyone there?

GRATIANO
There is some horror in the air,
An injured man.

LODOVICO
    What can be done?

RODERIGO
I cannot move.

LODOVICO
    [Surprised] There's more than one.

GRATIANO
There's two at least. It was some scrap.

LODOVICO
Let's wait for help. It could be a trap.

        [IAGO enters.]

IAGO
[to CASSIO] What is this?

CASSIO
    I'm crippled I fear

LODOVICO
That's Othello's man.

CASSIO
    Thank God you are here.
Some robbers attacked, I know not why.
I think that one lies hurt nearby.

IAGO
And who stands there? Give me a hand!

RODERIGO
And help me here.

CASSIO
[Indicating RODERIGO] That's one of the band!

IAGO
[Approaching RODERIGO] Your murdering dog!

[He stabs RODERIGO.]

RODERIGO
    You inhuman hound.

IAGO
Murderers lying dead on the ground.
In this sleepy town, a killing spree.
[Noticing LODOVICO and GRATIANO] Friend or foe?

LODOVICO
    Well . . . you tell me.

IAGO
Lodovico, Cassio's hurt!

CASSIO
Half my leg lies in the dirt!

GRATIANO
Cassio!

LODOVICO
 Cassio?

IAGO
 Bring me some light.
I'll bind your leg with my shirt real tight.

 [BIANCA enters.]

BIANCA
From whence do come these terrible cries?
[Noticing CASSIO] My Cassio! God, please strike my eyes!

IAGO
[to BIANCA] Stay back, you strumpet. Give him some
 space.
[to CASSIO] Your assailant, did you see his face?

CASSIO
I didn't, no.

BIANCA
 Something's amiss.

IAGO

I believe this whore had a hand in this.
This man I killed, let's see his face.
Roderigo!

GRATIANO

Roderigo!

IAGO

You know him, your Grace?

GRATIANO

I'm sad to say I'm afraid I do.

IAGO

And I'm sorry for ignoring you,
But what with all this chaos here . . .

GRATIANO

I quite understand; you've nothing to fear.

IAGO

Someone bring a stretcher out!

BIANCA

Cassio, my Cassio!

IAGO

There's no need to shout!
[To CASSIO] The man who's dead is Roderigo.
Was he your enemy?

CASSIO

I really don't know.

[Two stretcher bearers bring in the stretcher for CASSIO.]

IAGO

Finally the stretcher's here.

Let's move this good man out of here.

[To BIANCA] Look how pale is her complexion.

There's something here of your infection.

Keep watching her; she's highly strung.

The guilty speak without a tongue.

[Enter EMILIA]

EMILIA

My husband? Here? I heard the shouts!

What is happening hereabouts?

Is someone hurt?

IAGO

Roderigo's dead!

He and some friends wanted Cassio's head.

EMILIA

Does Cassio live?

IAGO

It's touch-and-go.

EMILIA

Oh dearest, dearest Cassio.

IAGO
Nothing good comes of visiting whores.
He ate his dinner behind your doors?

BIANCA
He ate with me.

IAGO
    You are involved!
Now come with me to get this solved.

EMILIA
You filthy strumpet, dirty whore.

BIANCO
I'm as moral as you, probably more!

IAGO
You both be quiet, you're making me stressed.
Make sure his wounds are properly dressed.

[Stretcher with CASSIO exuents.]

[To BIANCA] You're coming with me
    [to EMILIA] What you've seen and you've heard
Go take to Othello; Tell him what has occurred.
[Aside] If I can get through tonight unbusted,
My grizzly plan will be done, if not dusted.[7]

[Exeunt]

---

7   "Done and dusted" is a British idiom that means completed or finished.

SCENE II.

In Desdemona's room

[DESDEMONA sleeps.]

OTHELLO
So now it is my solemn duty
To kill my wife, this sleeping beauty.
Laid here she looks so innocent
But only death can now prevent
Continuing with her deceit,
And once she's gone there's no repeat.
An angel here from heaven sent,
Just one more kiss, so sweet a scent.
And now I am a heavenly host.
I kill what I do love the most.
And now she wakes . . .

DESDEMONA
    My love, you're there.

OTHELLO
I'll wait for you to say a prayer.

DESDEMONA
I did before I went to bed.

OTHELLO
Now say one more before you're dead.

DESDEMONA
You're killing me?

OTHELLO
　　I am.

DESDEMONA
　　　　But why?
For loving too much?

OTHELLO
You have to die!

DESDEMONA
I don't understand this need for grief.

OTHELLO
You gave away your handkerchief!

DESDEMONA
I lost it and Cassio did but find.

OTHELLO
He said you had sex.

DESDEMONA
　　Are you out of your mind?
He would never say that, and I am no whore.

OTHELLO
Well thanks to Iago, he'll say it no more.

DESDEMONA
You're saying he's dead?

OTHELLO
  He's had his fun.

DESDEMONA
He was deceived! And I'm undone!

OTHELLO
You cry for him? You little whore!

DESDEMONA
Just send me to another shore.
Or let me live just one more night.

OTHELLO
You will die now; don't put up a fight.
I cannot stop.

DESDEMONA
  Then just one prayer.

OTHELLO
It is too late.

EMILIA
[Calling from off] Is somebody there?

OTHELLO
[Smothering DESDEMONA] Why won't you die? What is
  wrong?
I don't want you to suffer long.

EMILIA

[From off] My Lord, my Lord.

OTHELLO

     Iago's wife!

Just as I did take her life,

She's here to say that Cassio's dead.

But wait, still movement in the bed.

[Removing the pillow from DESDEMONA's face] And now,
     she's gone. What have I done?

Let the moon block out the sun.

EMILIA

[From off] Othello please! Show thy face!

        [OTHELLO closes the curtain and unlocks the
               door. Emilia enters.]

Some foul deeds have taken place.

Roderigo was by Cassio slain.

OTHELLO

The plan's gone wrong, now that is plain.

DESDEMONA

Help me! I have been murdered here.

EMILIA

Is that Desdemona? The voice is not clear.

     [EMILIA pulls back the curtain from around the bed.]

My lady dear . . .

DESDEMONA
> *[Very weak]* They've murdered me.

OTHELLO
What is this hideous sight I see?

EMILIA
Who did this thing?

DESDEMONA
> I caused my own death.
I love my husband 'til my final breath.

> *[DESDEMONA dies.]*

EMILIA
She took her own life? I cannot concur.
A sin such as that would not come from her,
But there was no one else here. I do not know how.

OTHELLO
I took my revenge for her breaking her vow.

EMILIA
Cheating on you?

OTHELLO
> Yes. Your husband told me.

EMILIA
My husband?

OTHELLO
And that's why I killed her, you see?

EMILIA
My husband?

OTHELLO
Yes. Iago. He told me the lot.

EMILIA
My husband?

OTHELLO
'My husband'. Is that all you have got?

EMILIA
You naïve fool . . .

OTHELLO
[Drawing his sword] You'll feel my wrath.

EMILIA
My husband is a psychopath
To tell you that; that's so untrue.
She only shared herself with you!
I'll tell the world you snuffed her out.

OTHELLO
You wouldn't dare.

EMILIA
Just hear me shout!
Othello has killed my mistress dead.

[Enter MONTANO, LODOVICO, and IAGO]

MONTANO
What's going on? Is it true what she said?

EMILIA
My husband, you villain, you said that her bed
She shared with Cassio, and now she is dead!

IAGO
I said what Othello thought to be true.

EMILIA
You made it all up. There's real evil in you!

LODOVICO
My cousin lies dead?

MONTANO
    Desdemona's been slain?

OTHELLO
And with my bare hands; I would do it again.

MONTANO
Your marriage it did kill her dad,
But at least he's missed this sight we've had.

OTHELLO
She was cursed with a soul of unbridled lust
And had sex with a soldier, her murder was just.
The handkerchief was the final straw.
It was everything honest Iago saw.

EMILIA

[to IAGO] You devilish cad.

IAGO

   I'm warning you.

EMILIA

Nothing that he said was true.

She lost the hanky. I gave it to him. *[Points to IAGO]*

Who wanted it for reasons grim

IAGO

Now say no more . . .

               [He draws his sword.]

MONTANO

   He draws his blade?

On his wife, this goodly maid?

EMILIA

And then my husband planted it

For Cassio to take the hit.

[To OTHELLO] He then began to bend your ear,

And you've now killed what you held most dear.

OTHELLO

       [Drawing his sword and approaching IAGO]

You evil swine, I'll take your life

A thousand times.

       [IAGO stabs EMILIA and runs out.]

LODOVICO
> He stabbed his wife.

EMILIA
Lay me down. The light goes dim.

MONTANO
And take Othello's sword from him.

> *[LODOVICO snatches OTHELLO's sword.]*

Let us prepare a devil's tomb.
Don't let Othello leave this room.

> *[MONTANO and GRATIANO exit.]*

EMILIA
A wreath made of willow I now, too, shall wear.
And your wife she was pure 'til her last gasp of air!

> *[She dies.]*

OTHELLO
They think that they with ease disarm
This General but I still can harm.

> *[Finding a dagger on his person]*

[Aside] I keep another blade about.
[Calling] Uncle, I am coming out.

GRATIANO
[From off] You try that, I will kill you dead

OTHELLO

Then you come here to me instead.

I am unarmed.

[GRAZIANO enters and OTHELLO immediately grabs him and points a dagger at his throat.]

I found a dagger,

BUT DO NOT FRET. [OTHELLO RELEASES GRAZIANO.] I'VE LOST MY SWAGGER.

Why back away from this fearsome' Moor?

One breath from you, I'll hit the floor.

[to DESDEMONA] Your alabaster skin still soft,

We will together ascend aloft.

Soon we will be at heaven's gates,

But you'll send me down to my hell that awaits.

In purgatory, I will never atone.

Eternally I'll remain alone.

Come take my eyes and hide this sight.

Throw me to my fiery plight.

I'll burn in hell for what I've done.

Desdemona, she has gone.

[LODOVICO and MONTANO enter with CASSIO on a stretcher and IAGO as a prisoner.]

LODOVICO

Bring them in and close the door.

Where's Othello?

OTHELLO

I am no more.

LODOVICO
We bring him back.

OTHELLO
  Satan is nigh.
If he's the Devil, he shall not die.

     [OTHELLO stabs IAGO.]

LODOVICO
Someone take that weapon away.

IAGO
[Injured] I live to fight another day.

OTHELLO
But it will be in agony,
Which is better than your death to me.

LODOVICO
You were lured in by this devil's bait.

OTHELLO
But I killed for honour, not from hate.

LODOVICO
The devil did confess his plan.
Did you to collude to kill this man? *[Pointing at CASSIO]*

OTHELLO
I did.

CASSIO

But why? It's unspeakably cruel.

OTHELLO

I know that now. I was played for a fool.

[To IAGO] Why would you manipulate me?

There is still so much that I don't see.

IAGO

You know what you know, my talking is done.

GRATIANO

The forthcoming torture will loosen your tongue.

LODOVICO

[To IAGO] Your letters on Roderigo's body we found

About how to put Cassio dead in the ground.

OTHELLO

You fiend.

CASSIO

You beast.

OTHELLO

That letter is grim.

LODOVICO

And a second one, this time from Roderigo to him,

Full of complaints he was about to expose.

So Iago did kill him to keep clean his nose.

OTHELLO
That explains his early demise.
Now, Cassio, admit your handkerchief lies.

CASSIO
I found it in my room somewhere.
Iago just told me he planted it there.

OTHELLO
Oh, what a fool I am!

CASSIO
     That's right!
And he got me drunk on your honeymoon night,
Then sent Roderigo to fight me too.

OTHELLO
And that's when I demoted you!

LODOVICO
Rod told me this before he died.
I hope that you are satisfied!
Othello, you will leave with us.
Cassio will rule Cyprus.
We will leave you, Iago, where you belong.
Just torture him well and make it last long.

OTHELLO
Just a word before you go;
I've always helped Venice, that you all know.
So when you tell my history
Try, at least, to be fair to me.

If you do, the future will tell
That I loved not wisely but too well!
I believed the lies about my girl.
In consequence, I lost my pearl.
Tell them of the tears I cry.
And also of the time when I
Grabbed a Turk for beating his miss
And slit his throat something like this.

[He cuts his own throat.]

LODOVICO
Did you ever see an action so gory?

GRATIANO
A fitting end to this horror story.

OTHELLO
I kissed you when I took your breath,
And now you take my kiss of death.

[Kisses DESDEMONA and dies next to her.]

CASSIO
He was noble enough to take his own life,
But I didn't know he had a knife.

LODOVICO
[To IAGO] You bloodthirsty dog, more cruel than the sea,
These bodies are yours, you've sickened me!
Gratiano, you've inherited
Othello's things; it's merited.

Now, Governor, I must depart,
And Iago's punishment you can start.
Decide the manner, I suggest that it's gory.
I'm back to Venice to tell the whole story.

[Exeunt all but IAGO]

Epilogue

IAGO

[Aside] Oh come on, have some sympathy.

My plan it worked out perfectly.

Apart from Cassio not being killed,

I really couldn't be more thrilled.

Ok, I've got some torture to face,

But that is hardly a disgrace,

Not for a clever fellow like me.

I'll find my way back to the top of the tree.

It may take some time and more innocent lives.

This play's called Othello, but it's me who survives!

More Drama Resources from Alphabet Publishing

Silly Shakespeare for Students by Paul Leonard Murray

A Midsummer Night's Dream
Macbeth
Pericles
Hamlet
Othello
Twelfth Night

Short Original Plays by Alice Savage

Just Desserts: A foodie drama about a chef gone bad

Introducing Rob: Lola's family loves her new boyfriend. Until they actually meet him

Colorado Ghost Story: Two exchange students get into trouble in the old West

Strange Medicine: Who decides what the truth is?

The Drama Book: Lesson Plans, Activities, and Scripts for the English Language Classroom: Everything you need to start doing theatre, drama games, or plays in your classroom

ISTD Coursebooks by Alice Savage

The Integrated Skills Through Drama coursebooks contain a complete curriculum built around an original one-act play. Aimed at intermediate learners, teenagers and older.

Her Own Worst Enemy: A serious comedy about choosing a major

Only the Best Intentions: A love triangle between a guy, a girl and a game

Rising Water: A stormy drama about what happens to people in a crisis

Alphabet
PUBLISHING

Alphabet Publishing is an independent publisher of creative and innovative educational material. All of our resources were conceived and created by teachers working in the classroom. We support our creators by giving them creative control and by sharing profits. Learn more about us and our resources at www.alphabetpublish.com

www.ingramcontent.com/pod-product-compliance
Lightning Source LLC
Chambersburg PA
CBHW021652120626
46545CB00002B/824